I0088639

Multicultural Conference
Planning Guide

Dr. Randie S. Gottlieb

Published by

UNITYWORKS

Multicultural Conference Planning Guide

by Randie S. Gottlieb, Ed.D.

ISBN: 978-1-942053-03-3

© 2025 UnityWorks LLC. First edition, 2016. All rights reserved.

All rights reserved. No part of this document may be reproduced or transmitted in any form or by any means without prior written permission from the publisher.

Copies: UnityWorks hereby grants permission to the purchaser of this book to make copies of individual pages as needed for the purpose of conference planning. Copyright information must clearly show on all copies. Scanning, large-scale reproduction, re-distribution, inclusion in other publications and commercial uses are not permitted.

Free download: Selected pages from this book are available as a free download from our website. These items are offered as a convenience to purchasers of the book. The PDF files may be photocopied, and the Word and Excel files may be edited to meet your local needs. See p. 1 for details.

Disclaimer: It is the responsibility of the user to determine the suitability of the materials and activities in this publication, and the associated downloaded items, to meet the user's particular needs and the needs of others involved. The user therefore agrees to hold the author and UnityWorks, along with its personnel, employees, agents, contractors or volunteers, harmless from any claims and/or litigation arising from or related thereto.

**If you find these materials useful,
please let others know about them.**

Thank you!

Available from www.UnityWorks.org

Edited by Steven E. Gottlieb, M.D.

All images used with permission.

All websites and references listed
are correct at the time of publication.

Published by UnityWorks LLC
Yakima, Washington, USA

See page 1 for your free download.

Praise for the Planning Guide

"After over two decades of planning Multicultural Conferences in our state, Randie Gottlieb's Multicultural Conference Planning Guide is long overdue! Covering the critical elements in organizing for this specialized event, this guide provides a practical, effective resource for the beginner as well as the seasoned multicultural conference planner. It's an important tool you'll use again and again!"

— Dr. Cynthia Rekdal, Founder and Executive Director
WA State Association for Multicultural Education (WSAME)

"Opportunities to gather, share resources, and collectivize on topics of multiculturalism, diversity, and social justice are needed now more than ever, but planning such conferences can be difficult, especially for the first-timer. I sure wish I had this guide when I first started planning conferences—thorough in detail, packed with user-friendly suggestions and resources, invaluable to any conference planner!"

— Kevin Kumashiro, Dean, University of San Francisco School of Education
Author, "Against Common Sense: Teaching and Learning toward Social Justice"

"The National Center for Race Amity holds as a core strategy the goal of placing proven resources and blueprints in the hands of everyday professionals and lay people to engage cross-racial/cross-cultural understanding. The Multicultural Conference Planning Guide is a prize tool to engage that tactic. Brilliant!"

— William H. "Smitty" Smith, Ed.D.
Founding Executive Director, National Center for Race Amity

"Dr. Gottlieb's Multicultural Conference Planning Guide is excellent! Colorful, easy to read and understand, packed full of stimulating and thought-provoking activities, time-tested from her experience in the field of multicultural education for over 20 years, this guide offers everything from conference theme ideas, to program activities, logistical considerations and more. For anyone interested in organizing a multicultural conference that will cultivate honest and meaningful exchanges through inspirational learning activities, this is one of the best investments you can make!"

— Maria D. Cuevas, ABD, Chican@ Studies & Sociology Instructor
Department of Social Sciences, Yakima Valley Community College

"Never doubt
that a small group
of thoughtful committed citizens
can change the world.

Indeed,
it is the only thing
that ever has."

Margaret Mead

Table of Contents

Introduction

UnityWorks is a non-profit educational organization whose mission is to promote understanding of the oneness of humanity, the value of diversity and the need for unity. We provide training, materials and support to empower organizations, communities and individuals to work towards creating a more unified, just and peaceful world.

Our School Program often includes an annual Multicultural Conference planned by the local UnityWorks Coordinator or Leadership Team. This conference is usually held in May (springtime in the Northern Hemisphere) since it is close to the end of the school year. The Conference provides an opportunity for UnityWorks site teams:

- To share best practices and strengthen their network of support

- To review progress and challenges in implementing their Diversity Action Plans

- To meet and welcome any new UnityWorks schools

- To enhance our common vision of multicultural education

- To consult on collaborative projects and plans for the coming year

The conference program might include a keynote speech or panel presentation, reports from each site team, a demonstration or display, workshops on topics of interest, group discussions, student cultural performances, lunch or refreshments, music, and inspiring life stories from selected participants.

This book, designed to assist with planning a local UnityWorks conference, is a useful tool for any group. It includes theme and program ideas, sample letters of invitation, fliers, schedules, handouts, recommendations for room setup, guidelines for moderators and presenters, registration instructions, a planning checklist, an evaluation form and other essential materials.

For a large event involving rented facilities, hotel and catering contracts, vendor displays, the review and selection of proposals from multiple speakers and more, you will need to start sooner and may wish to have two planning groups: one for logistics and another for program development.

For additional materials designed to promote understanding of the oneness of humanity, the value of diversity and the need for unity, please visit our website: www.unityworks.org.

Free download: Your purchase of this book includes selected pages in an MS Word file including a sample flier, welcome sign and conference program, so they can be edited to meet your needs. Visit < www.unityworks.org/MCPGDL >.

Conference Planning

Conference Theme

A well-chosen conference theme can help unify the program and provide a focus for your efforts. If the theme aligns with the conference goals, it will serve as an umbrella concept under which the agenda, speakers, invitations, fliers, decorations, music, refreshments, giveaway items and all other activities and materials are made more coherent, memorable and effective. Presenters can also be asked to include a story, an example, or language that reinforces this centerpiece idea. Local history and customs might provide some thematic ideas. Examples of themes from previous conferences are listed below.

"Our Stories"

The goal of this conference was to demonstrate that sharing our personal histories can increase understanding and create bridges between those of different backgrounds. Our keynote speaker highlighted the need to show respect for others by truly listening to their stories, with the intention of understanding the life and worth of another person. Such careful listening, she said, can open a window onto the sacred and allow us to reach the depths, rather than just skimming the surface. This is how we should relate to those we teach—not on a superficial level, but with the deepest respect. If we do this, our students (regardless of age, gender, ethnicity, language or ability level) will feel that they belong.

"Talking the Talk"

This conference included sessions on working with English language learners, Native American oral traditions, the power of language, and responding to biased remarks. It closed with a recitation of student poetry in both English and Spanish, on various diversity themes.

"My Piece of the Puzzle"

This conference focused on the part we play individually and collectively in fostering multicultural attitudes and practices in our schools.

"The Sand in the Oyster: Creating Our Own Pearls"

This event was designed to help site teams learn how to create "pearls" when encountering resistance to their efforts. Like the sand in the oyster, these "irritating grains" can serve as a catalyst, providing new opportunities to learn and to promote growth from within.

"Planting Seeds of Hope: Nurturing Multicultural Learning"

This conference emphasized the importance of a grassroots approach—with site teams designing their own agendas for change. Like the seed, our multicultural goals and programs should start small and grow organically as capacity is built and resources become available. If the seed is to grow tall and strong, it will require ongoing care: water, fertilizer, weeding and sufficient sunlight.

In a moving ceremony at the close of the conference, each participant was asked to think of a personal action they could take to plant seeds of understanding or to nurture their team's Diversity Action Plan during the coming year. They then wrote their pledge on a brightly-colored sticky note, read aloud what they had written, and added it to a large flower poster that was "blooming" with each new "petal" at the front of the room. When turning in their evaluation forms, these "gardeners" also received a small seed packet as a reminder of their pledge.

"Ripples of Hope"

This letter was included in the conference handout packet and highlights another theme.

Dear friends,

We are delighted to welcome you to our second annual Spring Multicultural Conference with its theme, "Ripples of Hope." Like a pebble dropped in a pond, a small positive action by even one individual can ripple outward to foster positive change throughout a classroom, a school, or an entire community. Sometimes these ripples appear to go unnoticed, but together they form part of a larger current of history. In the words of Robert F. Kennedy:

Few will have the greatness to bend history itself,
but each of us can work to change a small portion of events,
and in the total of all those acts will be written
the history of this generation.

Each time a man* stands up for an ideal,
or acts to improve the lot of others,
or strikes out against injustice, he sends forth a tiny ripple of hope,
and crossing each other from a million different centers
of energy and daring, those ripples build a current
which can sweep down the mightiest walls
of oppression and resistance.

Our hope is that today's presentations and the opportunity to network with like-minded colleagues, will inspire *us* with hope, provide us with new ideas, and motivate us to create our own ripples of change. May we free ourselves, our schools and communities from the strong undertow of prejudice, resist the rising tide of fear and intolerance, and rise above the destructive flood of anger and violence. May we collectively strive to build bridges of unity and understanding, and work to foster positive multicultural change in our city and beyond.

We welcome you and hope you enjoy the conference!

Randie Gottlieb, President
UnityWorks Foundation

* If Robert Kennedy were speaking to us today, no doubt he would have said,
   "Each time a *person* stands up..." We have preserved his original wording from 1966.

Some Program Ideas

The Spring Conference should be designed to meet the evolving needs of the UnityWorks Program in your area. It can be as simple as an afternoon meeting where the participants have an opportunity to discuss what they have been learning during the year and to make suggestions for the future. As the Program grows, the Conference might become an all-day event—perhaps open to the public, or it could eventually develop into a popular weekend retreat and showcase—with keynote speakers, panel discussions, catered meals, outdoor activities and an array of cultural performances.

Some program ideas that you may wish to consider are listed below:

- Official welcome
- Opening ceremony
- Introduction of Leadership Team, site teams and special guests
- Recognition of hosts and sponsors
- Warm-up activities related to the theme
- Keynote speaker
- Team presentations on their activities from the previous year
- Panel discussion (e.g. a presentation by teachers or students from different schools)
- My Story presentations (see p. 47)
- Displays of multicultural books, student artwork, items for sale
- Demonstrations (e.g. "My Best Multicultural Lesson")
- Video or PowerPoint showing UnityWorks activities from the past year
- Workshops on topics suggested by UnityWorks site team leaders
  (Previous workshops have included: Working with ELL Students, Handling Conflict in the Classroom, The Power of Language, Teacher Expectations and Student Achievement, Differential Discipline, Honoring Our Ancestors, Involving Parents and Community, Responding to Biased Remarks)
- Student performances (music, drumming, dance, drama, poetry)
- Time for collaborative project development
- Group discussion on challenging issues
- Music, singing, cooperative games
- Question and answer session
- Meals and snack breaks
- Video screenings
- Group photo
- Presentation of any awards or scholarships
- Door prizes (to bring people back quickly after breaks)
- Free time and recreational activities (nature hike, yoga, crafts)
- Announcements of upcoming local UnityWorks events
- Conference evaluation and closing ceremony

Mixed Group Activities

In addition to spending time with their own teams, the participants might be grouped into mixed teams for a variety of purposes. Two examples are given below.

Warm-up Activities

In order to "break the ice" and facilitate networking across teams, you might decide to plan one or more warm-up activities. One easy way to quickly divide people into mixed groups for such activities is to provide name tags with different-colored stickers and matching table tents.

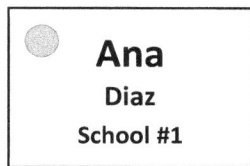

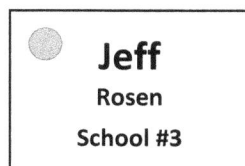

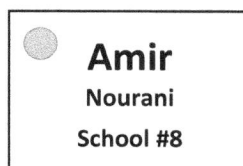

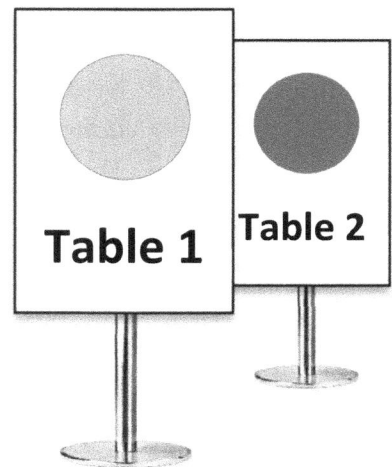

Make sure that each group is composed of people from different site teams. Stickers can be added randomly, or strategically to put specific groups of people together.

Collaborative Project Development

When the UnityWorks Program is first established in a particular area, activities will likely focus on individual schools and be organized separately by each site team. As the Program grows, the teams will often identify areas of common interest, and they may wish to share resources or develop collaborative projects involving two or more schools.

Suggestions for joint projects can be brainstormed during the conference or submitted beforehand. During the conference, for example, participants can be given index cards or large sticky notes, then asked to write down topics they wish to discuss. The cards can then be posted in a "marketplace of ideas" along the wall. During a break, conference organizers can group similar topics, list them on the board, and ask participants to vote for the top four or five.

Topics receiving the most votes can each be assigned to a different table, and teams can send one or more representatives to those tables based on interest. Each group should be asked to appoint a moderator and a recorder, and any resulting plans or proposals can be shared with the entire group at the end.

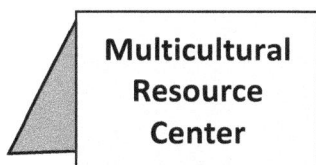

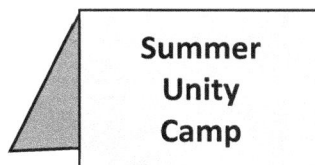

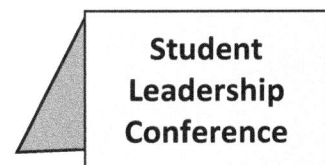

Budget

The planning team should list all the items needed to successfully carry out the conference. These items might be provided by the school district or other host organization, contributed by local sponsors, or covered by registration fees. Income and expenses should match since the Spring Conference is not intended as a profit-making venture. A budget for the event might include some of the following:

- Printing and postage
- Facility and audiovisual equipment rental
- Food including beverage service, meals, snacks, paper goods
- Photocopies, lamination, nametags, folders, markers and other supplies
- Keynote speaker honorarium including reimbursement for travel expenses
- Banners, flowers, tablecloths, centerpieces and other decorations
- Thank-you gifts, awards, door prizes, souvenirs
- Miscellaneous expenses

Sample Budget

Income
Grants and donations	500.00
In-kind contributions	200.00
Registration fees ($10 x 30)	300.00
TOTAL INCOME	**$1,000.00**

Expenses
Food	500.00
Hall and AV rental	-0-
Printing and postage	150.00
Registration packets, supplies	100.00
Keynote speaker	250.00
TOTAL EXPENSES	**$1,000.00**

Room Setup

The room set-up is important to the overall tone and success of the meeting. Tables, chairs, sound, temperature, lighting, background music, stage, space for breakout sessions—all play a role. See diagram on the following page. You will also want to check with the facility to arrange for any audiovisual equipment you might need, for example:

☐ Digital projector with a laptop cable and screen

☐ Flip chart or whiteboard with markers and eraser

☐ Sound system including microphone for large rooms

☐ Power strip and/or extension cords

If you plan to use the Internet, check with the facility beforehand to be sure there is an Ethernet cable or Wi-Fi connection, and that you have the password if necessary. In addition, check each website that you plan to visit to confirm that there are no filters blocking access. In many school districts, for example, outside presenters cannot access YouTube or other social media platforms.

Prepare some upbeat music in advance, tied into the conference theme if possible, and have it playing during breaks and when people first enter the room.

Microphone Setup

In most cases, the venue will handle all audio arrangements. However, if you do need to set up a microphone, you will want to familiarize yourself with how to adjust the height and angle, how to remove and replace the mic in its holder, how to adjust the volume, and how to turn it on and off.

You will also want to prevent audio feedback—that unpleasant screeching noise caused by sound traveling from the mic to the amplifier and back through the mic to create a sound loop. With a portable sound system, place the amplifier between the microphone and the audience, i.e. stay behind the amplifier. (See diagram below.) Be sure the mic is not too close to the amplifier or it could still cause interference. With a permanently installed system, you should be able to place the mic anywhere.

Wrong amplifier placement   **Correct amplifier placement**

Sample Room Setup

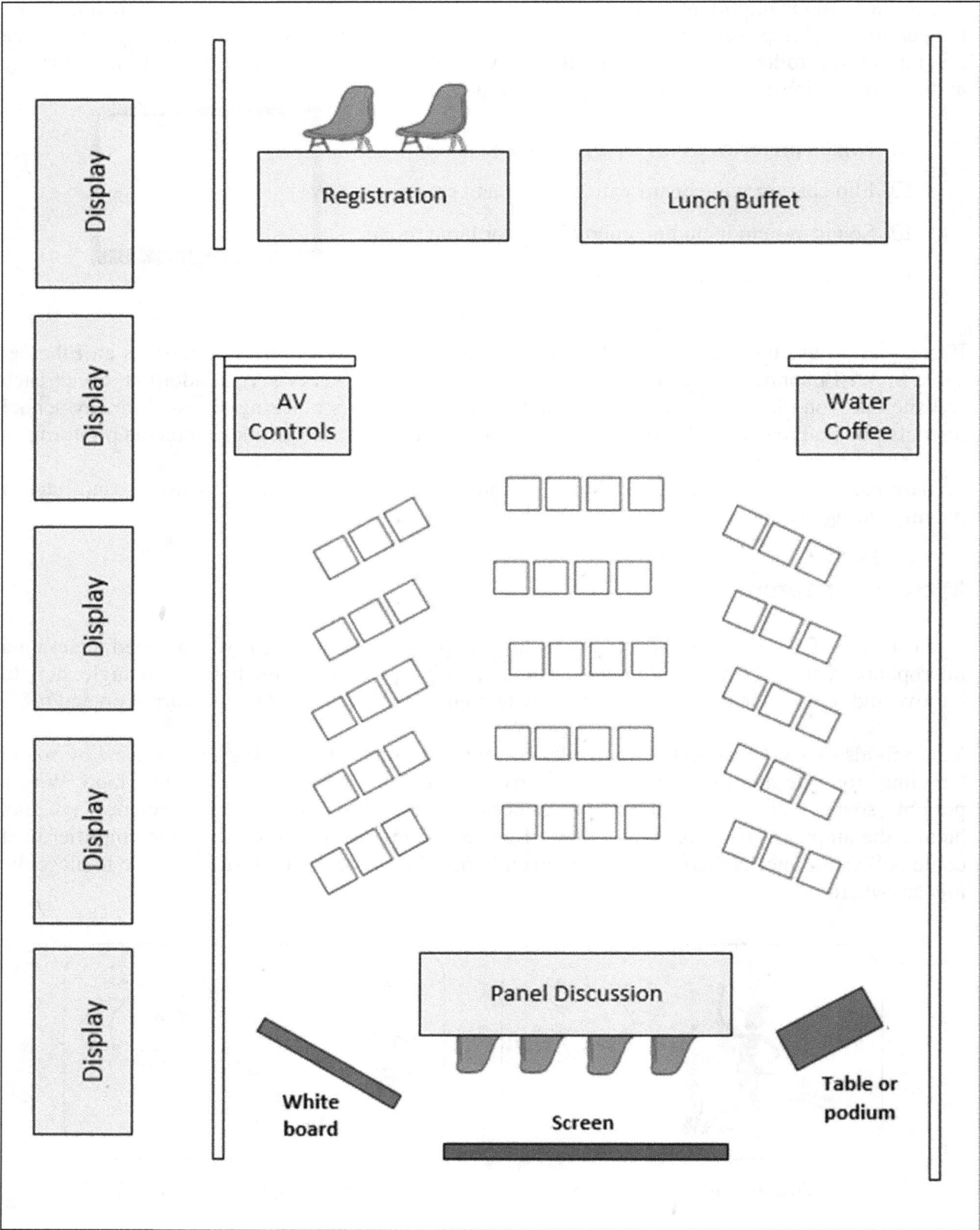

Display (×5, left wall)

Registration

Lunch Buffet

AV Controls

Water Coffee

Panel Discussion

White board

Screen

Table or podium

Seating

To maximize energy in the room, close air walls to tighten the space, limit the number of chairs and place the first row about five feet from the speaker. Encourage people to fill up the front first by placing "reserved" signs at the back tables or use masking tape to restrict access to the back rows. A huge room with empty seats, especially near the front, will make it harder for the speaker to connect with the audience. You can always open up the back rows or add more chairs if needed.

Chairs should be about six inches apart and staggered, rather than lined up right behind each other, so people aren't wedged together or blocked by a tall person sitting directly in front of them. Curve the outside rows in and angle the chairs towards the presenter so members of the audience can also see each other. For groups larger than 50 or seating more than five rows deep, you may need a riser or stage area so the speaker can easily be seen.

If possible, avoid a middle aisle as it creates two audiences and leaves the speaker facing an empty space. If you are showing a PowerPoint or video, it's best to use a ceiling mount or rear projection system to avoid having to create a center aisle just for the projector table.

Meals and Refreshments

If food and beverages will be served, consider the following suggestions:

1. Have a buffet line using both sides of a long table so people can pick up their food more quickly. With a double line, you will need two sets of serving utensils.

2. Give the line a starting point, an ending point, and an obvious flow: e.g., plates at the beginning, spoons and forks at the end. Put out two sets of each item, and have napkins available in several places in case of drips and spills.

3. Arrange the food table strategically, with the most plentiful or least expensive food first. Use smaller serving spoons or toothpicks for scarcer items to imply portion control.

4. Use signs to indicate what the food is (especially important for those with food allergies), and label vegetarian, vegan or gluten-free options.

5. Put drinks at a separate table in another part of the room so people can fill their cups without holding up the buffet line. If possible, put the beverage table close to the kitchen to make it easier to re-fill coffee pots and jugs of water.

6. Don't forget the trash cans.

Signs, Name Tags and Forms

Clear signage can help to identify the event, direct people to breakout rooms, highlight displays, and generally help make the conference flow more smoothly. The following signs and table tents are included in color with the free download for purchasers of this book (see p.1 for details).

Welcome!

UnityWorks

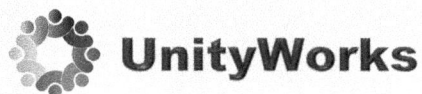

Spring Multicultural Conference

"Planting Seeds of Hope: Nurturing Multicultural Learning"

**These directional signs can be printed on card stock,
cut on the solid lines, and posted on the walls as needed.**

UnityWorks

Spring
Multicultural
Conference

UnityWorks

Spring
Multicultural
Conference

⬅️

UnityWorks

Spring
Multicultural
Conference

➡️

The following signs can be printed on card stock, cut on the solid lines, and folded back on the dotted lines as indicated to form table tents.

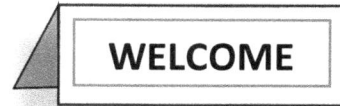

WELCOME

WELCOME
We're glad you're here!

REGISTRATION
Please Sign In

CLOCK HOURS

AGENDAS

NAME TAGS

HANDOUTS
Take One of Each

EVALUATIONS

Name Tags

Name tags should have a first name large enough to read easily, and include the person's institutional affiliation (see examples below). You will also want to bring some blank name tags and markers.

Registration List

A pre-registration list can be used to generate the sign in sheet, meal count, media release forms, clock hour list and name tags. If fees will be charged, you will also need to keep track of who has paid. An Excel sheet (see sample below) can be customized to meet your needs. Also see registration instructions on p. 40.

	Last	First	School/Org	Position	Email	Phone	Fee	Paid	Check/Cash
1	Alvarez	Maria	Lincoln MS	Librarian	maria@lms	987-6543	$10.00	$10.00	#3571
2	Shevin	Beth	UnityWorks	Board	beth@uwf	654-3210	---	---	guest
3									
4									
5									

Media Release Form

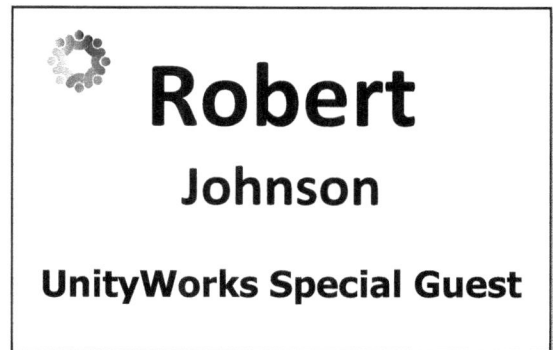

A sample media release form is included on the following page, and is also part of the download packet. Names from the registration list can be added in alphabetical order prior to the event in order to speed up the signing process.

Participants who do not want to be photographed, can be given a nametag sticker (e.g. a small red dot), so the photographer will be aware of their wishes.

Media Release

Permission to Use Audio, Video and Photographs

I hereby give permission for UnityWorks and its representatives, to take audio or video recordings or photographs of me, to be used on the UnityWorks website, and in any teacher's guides, PowerPoint programs or other educational resources, and in any promotional materials in connection with these items. I agree that UnityWorks, its assigns and transferees may copyright, publish and use these materials, in whole or in part, separately or in conjunction with other media, with or without my name, in print and electronically, for any lawful purpose.

UNITYWORKS
www.unityworks.org

I have read and understand the above, and give my consent freely and without reservation.

	Print Name	Signature	Print Email	Phone
1				
2				
3				
4				
5				
6				
7				
8				
9				
10				
11				
12				
13				
14				
15				
16				
17				
18				
19				
20				
21				
22				
23				
24				
25				
26				
27				
28				
29				
30				

Conference Planning Checklist

Select from this list as appropriate for your event and assign someone to each task.

5-6 Months Before

[ ] Appoint a planning committee and/or coordinator for the event
[ ] Set a conference date and times [A]
[ ] Decide on a minimum and maximum number of participants [B]
[ ] Select and reserve a suitable facility that is ADA compliant and accessible to transportation [C]
[ ] Add to school district calendar and ask site teams to save the date
[ ] Obtain local sponsors if needed

3-4 Months Before

[ ] Determine conference theme
[ ] Develop the program and schedule
[ ] Select MC and keynote speaker
[ ] Invite additional presenters and performers, or send out a request for proposals if desired [D]
[ ] Reserve any AV equipment as needed for each presentation, including extension cords
[ ] Prepare budget (hall rental, food, photocopies, nametags, supplies, speaker honorarium, etc.)
[ ] Determine if fees will be charged and if so, how much, or how funds will be raised [B]
[ ] Create a flier, PSA, registration form and other publicity materials as needed
[ ] Invite teams, sponsors and special guests [E]
[ ] Submit clock hour request

1-2 Months Before

[ ] Confirm and orient MC, presenters and performers
[ ] Obtain title and description for each presentation, along with brief presenter bios
[ ] Send "My Story" guidelines to all who will be sharing their personal stories (p. 48)
[ ] Remind teams and continue publicizing the event to ensure good attendance
[ ] Prepare registration list or spreadsheet with each participant's name, school/org, email/phone [F]
[ ] Ask each team, or selected teams, to put together a brief presentation on their activities to date
[ ] Ask site team leaders to submit suggestions for collaborative projects
[ ] Make housing and transportation arrangements for out of town presenters and guests
[ ] Arrange for coffee/tea, meals and snacks, keeping possible dietary restrictions in mind
[ ] Design and order conference banner, posters, and other decorations
[ ] Arrange to have photos or videos taken
[ ] Assign a door prize coordinator and begin collecting door prizes
[ ] Confirm clock hour approval and obtain official sign-in forms
[ ] Order or prepare any items for sale (books, T-shirts, etc.) and arrange for someone to handle sales
[ ] Create any handouts, PowerPoint slides, conference program, song sheets, media release forms, etc.

A. Avoid conflict with cultural and religious holidays, other school district meetings and major civic events.
B. You might also decide on a maximum number per team, or charge for additional team members and for the public.
C. Consider the number of participants and the type of activities planned. See Room Setup (p. 9-11) for suggestions.
D. Choose speakers from a diversity of backgrounds with expertise in the topic, including students, parents and community members who might bring a unique perspective.
E. Special guests might include school board members, superintendents, local legislators, representatives from Rotary or other service clubs, cultural organizations, colleges, media outlets, interfaith councils and community groups.
F. The list might be organized by category, e.g. conference planners, site teams, sponsors, presenters, special guests.

1-2 Weeks Before
[ ]   Send a reminder to presenters and key personnel with time, date, room assignments
[ ]   Make signs and posters: welcome, this way, registration, clock hours, take one, etc.
[ ]   Appoint door greeters and registrars (students might be enlisted for this service)
[ ]   Assign specific individuals to greet and accompany any special guests who plan to attend
[ ]   Assign someone to briefly introduce each workshop presenter
[ ]   Orient registrars, sponsor hosts and workshop introducers
[ ]   Add any PPTs to laptop and confirm all audiovisual equipment with the venue
[ ]   Prepare small gifts and/or thank-you cards for presenters and sponsors
[ ]   Finalize registration list and send letter of confirmation to all participants
[ ]   Obtain small stickers (e.g. a red dot) for nametags of those who don't want their photo taken
[ ]   Prepare a brief evaluation form and obtain a box or folder for collecting the forms
[ ]   Prepare small prizes as an incentive for turning in the evaluations

A Few Days Before
[ ]   Confirm any arrangements for photography, catering, refrigeration, etc.
[ ]   Prepare name tags, sign-in lists, clock hour forms, media releases, table signs, etc.
[ ]   Add matching stickers to name tags and table cards if grouping people for mixed-team activities
[ ]   Obtain paper cups, plates, napkins, flowers, tablecloths or other decorations
[ ]   Prepare numbered tickets or cut up a list of participants and put in a box for door prize selection
[ ]   Copy handouts, prepare registration packets, add folder labels, laminate signs
[ ]   Prepare list of announcements (turn off cell phones, location of restrooms, etc.)

Same Day or Day Before
[ ]   Bring laptop, camera, room diagram, tape, tacks, clipboards, paper, pens, marker, stapler, scissors+
[ ]   Set up room (tables, chairs, projector, screen, audio, whiteboard, flip chart, easels, food, etc.)
[ ]   Set up registration area (sign-in sheets, name tags, media releases, clock hour forms, programs, etc.)
[ ]   Post signs and banners, set out handouts, arrange displays (including UW books and brochures)
[ ]   Put "reserved" signs on selected tables
[ ]   At the end of the program, give out door prizes and collect evaluations

After the Event
[ ]   Sign and submit clock hour forms, make any payments and prepare invoices as needed
[ ]   Send thank-you notes to presenters, volunteers, hosts and others as appropriate
[ ]   Send a brief report with photos to the host organization, sponsors, site teams, local media, etc.
[ ]   Review and compile evaluations and use to inform future planning
[ ]   Schedule a massage!

Sample Documents

Sample Schedules

Half Day Schedule

11:30 Check-in and working lunch (How is UnityWorks functioning at our school?)
12:00 Welcome and introductions: Ms. Amber Brown, UnityWorks District Coordinator
12:05 Part of Your World, sung by Jasmine Chen, Lincoln Elementary School student
12:10 Keynote: Dr. Alexa Smith, President of Harmony University, "Planting Seeds of Hope"
12:30 Team mixer warm-up activity (word puzzles)
12:45 Site team presentations (share progress on Diversity Action Plans - 5 min. each)
 1:15 Whole group and site team photos
 1:30 Refreshments
 1:45 Song: "Listen" by Red Grammer
 1:50 Closing the Achievement Gap: Mr. Ted Johnson, Principal, MLK Middle School
 2:05 My Story: Ms. Mary Whitehorse, Librarian, Union Tribal School
 2:35 My Story: Mr. Luis Rivera Flores, Sociology Professor, YVCC
 3:05 Upcoming events and next steps
 3:15 Davis High School Jazz Choir
 3:30 Conference ends

Full Day Schedule

 8:00 Registration and coffee
 8:30 Welcome and introductions
 8:35 Opening ceremony by drummers and dancers from the Tribal School
 8:50 Keynote address
 9:05 Team mixer warm-up activity (Unity Bingo)
 9:20 Selected site team presentations (10 min. each)
10:25 Whole group and site team photos
10:40 Break with refreshments
10:55 Workshop options and announcements
11:00 Concurrent workshops (choose one)
   ➢ Track 1: Students
   ➢ Track 2: Educators
   ➢ Track 3: Community
12:00 Lunch
12:45 Speaker: My Best Multicultural Lesson
 1:00 My Story presentations (30 min. each)
 2:00 Break with refreshments
 2:15 Plenary session (panel, challenging issues, video, discussion) or team planning time
 3:05 Upcoming events, next steps and takeaways
 3:15 Performance by the Yakima Children's Choir
 3:30 Conference ends

Note: Be aware of cultural differences with regard to time. In order to start when scheduled, it is helpful to include time for check-in and socializing at the beginning of the event, and to note on the invitation that the conference will begin promptly at the specified time.

Two-Day Schedule

This could be held in town or at a nearby retreat center on a weekend.

Day 1 - Evening
4:30	Registration (coffee and juice available)
4:55	Conference opening, welcome and introductions
5:00	Student musical performance
5:15	Keynote address
5:30	Dinner and recognition of UnityWorks sponsors
6:30	Group photo
6:45	Panel presentation or video with discussion
7:30	Free time and social activities

Day 2 - Morning
7:15	Morning hike or yoga (7:15-8:00)
7:30	Breakfast (7:30-8:30)
8:35	Announcements and questions
8:40	Speaker: My Best Multicultural Lesson
9:00	Team mixer warm-up activity
9:15	Selected site team presentations (15 min. each)
10:15	Break with refreshments
10:45	Concurrent workshops (breakout rooms)

Day 2 - Afternoon
11:45	Lunch
12:30	Challenging issues and questions (mixed team activity)
1:15	My Story presentations (30 min. each)
2:15	Team time and collaborative project development (rolling break)
3:10	Upcoming events and next steps
3:15	Retreat evaluation and closing activity
3:30	Lodge check out

Valerie Kanu, Davis High School parent, and Verlynn Best, President and CEO of the Yakima Chamber of Commerce, during the first UnityWorks Spring Conference in Yakima, WA, 2015

Sample Flier

UnityWorks

Spring Multicultural Conference

For UnityWorks Site Teams and Invited Guests

"Planting Seeds of Hope:
Nurturing Multicultural Learning"

**Thursday, May 28, 11:30-3:30
Yakima School District Office**

With appreciation to our sponsors:
Yakima School District, Rabbani Trust,
Yakima Valley Community Foundation

Keynote by
Dr. Alexa Smith
HU President

UnityWorks
Site Team
Presentations

Our Stories

Davis High School
Jazz Choir

Lunch Included

Clock Hours
Available

Please RSVP
by April 28

For information
about UnityWorks:

www.unityworks.org

To register:

Lucas Ortiz
(206) 865-1234

OrtizLucas
@ysd.org

Sample Program

UnityWorks
Spring Conference

For UnityWorks Site Teams, Thursday, May 28

Thank you to the Yakima School District and Rabbani Trust

"Planting Seeds of Hope:
Nurturing Multicultural Learning"

Purpose

- An annual opportunity for UnityWorks site teams to network and share best practices
- To review progress and challenges in implementing our Diversity Action Plans
- To showcase our efforts for representatives from potential new schools
- To consult on any collaborative projects and other suggestions for next year
- To enrich our common vision of multicultural education

Program

11:30	Check in and working lunch: How is UnityWorks making a difference at our school?
12:00	Welcome: Ms. Amber Brown, UnityWorks District Coordinator
12:05	Part of Your World, sung by Jasmine Chen, Lincoln Elementary student
12:10	Keynote: Dr. Alexa Smith, HU President, "Planting Seeds of Hope"
12:30	Team mixer warm-up activity
12:45	Site team presentations and panel discussion
1:30	Refreshments, whole group and site team photos
1:45	Unity song: "Listen" by Red Grammer
1:50	Closing the Achievement Gap: Mr. Ted Johnson, Principal, MLK Middle School
2:05	My Story: Ms. Mary Whitehorse, Librarian, Union Tribal School
2:35	My Story: Mr. Luis Rivera Flores, Sociology Professor, YVCC
3:05	Upcoming events and next steps
3:15	Davis High School Jazz Choir
3:30	Conference ends

**Please fill out a conference evaluation
and a clock hour form before you leave.**

For more info: www.unityworks.org

To join the program:
Lucas Ortiz, (206) 865-1234

To sponsor a school:
Dr. Sara Azadeh, (206) 865-1000

Handouts

Handouts can be placed in front of a "Take One" sign on the registration table, stuffed into folders which are distributed to the participants, or stapled and left in a stack at each table. You may wish to include some of the following:

- Conference agenda
- Contact list for local UnityWorks teams
- Letter of welcome relating to conference theme (p. 5)
- UnityWorks Program Overview for new team members and special guests (p. 29-30)
- Highlights of UnityWorks activities from previous years.
- Handouts needed for any warm-up activities
- Descriptions of any collaborative proposals with relevant contact info
- Flier for UnityWorks Summer Diversity Training Institute
- Multicultural resources list
- Song sheets
- Evaluation forms (p. 50)

Folder Labels

If participants will be given folders for their handouts, you may wish to add a sticky label to the front of each folder (see sample below).

UnityWorks Conference
Town, Date

UNITYWORKS
School Program

www.unityworks.org > Programs

Our Mission: UnityWorks is a nonprofit educational organization committed to a belief in the oneness of humanity, the value of diversity and the need for unity. Our mission is to reduce prejudice, and to promote cross-racial and cross-cultural understanding, equity and inclusion, with a focus on K-12 schools.

We work with educators and community leaders, providing diversity training, resources and ongoing support—with the goal of building local capacity for positive multicultural change.

Education is one of the most powerful factors in determining whether people reach their potential. Yet even with the best educational practices and materials, we won't achieve our academic goals without culturally-responsive classrooms and equitable, inclusive schools. Awareness and good intentions are not enough. We need concrete knowledge, practical skills, resources, moral courage and the will to act. The mission of UnityWorks is to address to this need.

School Program: Involvement in the Program begins with an intensive five-day Summer Training Institute for site teams from each participating school. This professional learning event (with clock hours available) is designed to prepare educators with the knowledge, tools, strategies and resources needed to improve school culture and student learning, and to develop and carry out a successful Diversity Action Plan.

Rather than mandating a set curriculum or asking schools to follow standardized directives from above, UnityWorks offers pro-active leadership with a grassroots approach that empowers each site team to design and implement its own blueprint for growth. We believe that building local capacity, and working together in teams within the context of a larger network of support, are critical for fostering sustainable change.

Program Organization: The UnityWorks School Program is organized on three levels:

1. Site Team: Designs and implements a Diversity Action Plan based on its own priorities

2. District Coordinator: Spearheads the local program and assists the site team at each school*

3. UnityWorks Foundation: Provides training, materials and ongoing support

> * If two or more schools from the same district wish to join, the district is asked to identify a staff member who will provide leadership and support for the participating site teams. The Coordinator may arrange for site visits, a spring conference and other local events.

Site Team Requirements

1. Each team should have at least four members: (A) an administrator; (B) a teacher; (C) a librarian, counselor or other staff member serving multiple grade levels; and (D) a parent or community representative. Teams may also include high school students if desired.

2. Teams must commit to attending the UnityWorks Training where they will develop an action plan.

3. Each team will meet regularly during the school year to carry out its plan, and will submit two feedback forms for the UnityWorks newsletter in October and June.

How Much Does it Cost?

- $5,000 per school for up to four people, with $1,000 for additional team members.
- Covers tuition for the weeklong Training Institute, quarterly newsletter, discounts on selected download materials, plus ongoing phone and email support for one school year.
- Each school is asked to provide a $1,000 budget directly to their site team for its Action Plan.

Educational Resources: UnityWorks also offers easy-to-use curriculum guides with step-by-step lesson plans; colorful PowerPoint programs for children on diversity, skin color and over-coming prejudice; conversation starter kits with guidelines and activities for facilitating constructive conversations on race; a School Climate Survey; a multicultural conference planning guide; and other resources. Visit us online: < www.unityworks.org> and click on Bookstore.

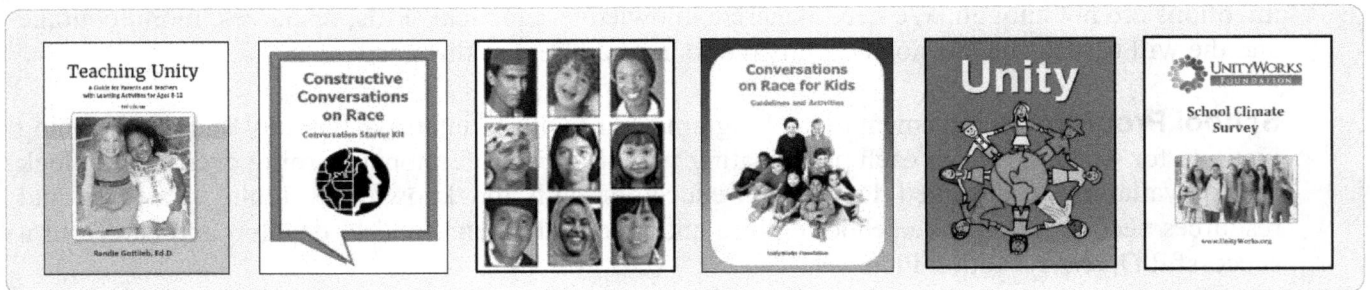

The Big Picture: Unity is one of the overarching needs of our time, yet it remains an elusive hope. How do we move beyond a fractured understanding of humanity and people-made barriers, to create a society where all feel welcome, where differences are valued and people are treated with justice, dignity and respect?

Rather than feeling powerless and discouraged in the face of recent events, UnityWorks believes that educators have an essential role to play in creating the future we wish to see. We may not be responsible for the past, but together we can take responsibility for our common destiny. In a world torn by injustice, hate and war, our classrooms can become models of hope for the future.

Join Us! If you are interested in establishing a UnityWorks Program in your school or district, you can download an application from our website. We look forward to working with you!

We Need Your Help! Make a strategic investment in your community by spreading the word about the UnityWorks Program and by contributing on our website. Every dollar makes a difference. With your generous support, together we can create positive and lasting social change.

Sample Letters to Participants

Invitation to Site Teams

* Team Leaders: please share with your team

Greetings friends,

UnityWorks is pleased to announce our first **Spring Multicultural Conference**, to be held on Thursday afternoon, May 28, from 11:30-3:30, beginning with lunch in Conference Room B at the Yakima School District Central Office, 123 N. 4th Street.

Conference Theme: Planting Seeds of Hope: Nurturing Multicultural Learning.

Objectives: The Conference will provide an opportunity for UnityWorks site teams to:

- Network and share best practices
- Review progress and challenges in implementing our Diversity Action Plans
- Showcase our efforts for representatives from interested new schools
- Consult on any collaborative projects and plans for the coming year

It will also be a chance to renew friendships, strengthen our network of support, and enhance our common vision of multicultural education

Registration: Your UnityWorks team may bring up to five members free of charge (lunch included). The enclosed flier shows the conference schedule. UnityWorks Administrative Assistant, Lucas Ortiz, will be contacting team leaders early next week to confirm who will be participating from each school.

What to Bring: Each team should prepare a five-minute presentation on your UnityWorks activities for the year. You can include any highlights, statistics, something your team is proud of, a goal achieved, a moving story, a lesson learned, a challenge that you are facing or one you have overcome, new insights gained, and any suggestions for next year. New teams can use the time to introduce their members and to share any hopes and plans.

In addition, your team should bring any items you wish to display, including photos of your UnityWorks activities, sample multicultural lessons or handouts, student work, recommended books, or other useful resources. Each team will have a small table to display these materials. All items should be labeled with your name and school. If you have handouts, bring 50 copies.

Clock Hours: Will be available through ESD 105 after the conference.

We look forward to seeing you on May 28th!

Warmly,
Your UnityWorks Team

As the annual conference grows in size, the invitation letter may include some additional information. See sample paragraphs below.

(1) You are also encouraged to invite additional staff and faculty, parents, high-school students, educational and cultural organizations, local service clubs, and other community groups and individuals who are interested in multicultural issues. The conference fee is $10 for each additional UnityWorks team member, $20 for other adults, and $5 for students. The enclosed flier contains basic information about the conference and an individual registration form.

(2) If you are attending for free as a member of your UnityWorks team, there is no need to complete an individual registration form. Just have your team leader submit a list of the five team members who plan to attend. This team list should be sent to OrtizLucas@ysd.org as soon as possible so your space can be reserved.

(3) Conference highlights will include an opening talk by Dr. Alexa Smith, President of Harmony University, a dramatic student presentation called "Circle of Hate," and the introduction of four new UnityWorks teams. In addition, we have planned an early morning hike and an evening of cooperative games.

(4) After dinner on Tuesday, each team will be asked to give a five-minute presentation about one multicultural activity from their project this past year. Whether the activity was successful or not, there is still something to be learned. Your team can either tell about the activity or demonstrate it, and include details so others will know how it's done. You are encouraged to use art, music, dance, drama, poetry, rap, pantomime, a puzzle, game or other creative means for your presentation. New schools can use the time to introduce their team members and to share any hopes, questions or goals.

(5) In addition, we are asking for one representative from each UnityWorks team to participate in the conference opening ceremony. The ceremony will include a brief readers' theater piece. Your representative will need to meet about 15 minutes before the start of the conference for a brief rehearsal. Please contact me with the name and contact information for your team rep.

(6) This year, we would like to start a curriculum bank of multicultural activities and lesson plans that will be available to all UnityWorks schools. If you have something that you wish to share, please send it to me by May 8th and it will be included in the handouts, or bring 75 copies with you to the retreat.

(7) Each team should prepare a three-minute presentation on "How Our School is Different Because of UnityWorks." We are hoping not for a list of activities, but specific changes you have seen in individuals, classrooms, school climate, or the community as a result of your efforts. This might include an increase in cross-cultural friendships or more positive interactions between students in general, a decrease in discipline referrals or biased remarks, improvement in academic achievement, more parent participation, fewer complaints about multicultural activities, a greater number of teachers indicating they have included multicultural content in their daily lessons, etc. Please share any data, anecdotes or observations you have as evidence of these changes

(8) For those who are interested, please bring proposals for collaborative projects that would involve two or more UnityWorks schools. We have scheduled time on Wednesday afternoon for consulting on your ideas. Previous proposals have included:

- Multicultural curriculum bank
- UnityWorks student service corps
- InterValley student ambassadors program
- Multicultural resource center for books and AV materials to be housed at the district office
- Theater group for plays written and produced by students on various diversity topics
- Summer unity camp run by teacher candidates from Harmony University
- Ongoing series of diversity workshops for staff and faculty
- Multicultural student leadership conference

(9) With regard to room and board, we will be making all the arrangements, so there is no need to contact the White Pass Lodge. Please let me know if you have any special dietary requirements or roommate requests, and inform me immediately if you must cancel, so we are not charged for your meals and lodging.

The retreat will be informal so dress comfortably. You might wish to bring sturdy walking shoes and a jacket for the cool mountain air. You are also welcome to bring musical instruments and a favorite game. Teams should arrive by 4:30 p.m. to register at the Lodge, then join us in the dining hall for coffee. The retreat is scheduled to begin promptly at 5:00 with opening remarks by Dr. Nakagawa. Please feel free to contact me with any questions. We look forward to seeing you at the Lodge!

(10) In closing, please remember to:

[ ]   Share this letter with your UnityWorks team.
[ ]   Contact Lucas Ortiz (509-865-1234 or OrtizLucas@ysd.org) with
      the names of up to five team members who will attend the conference.
[ ]   Indicate any dietary requirements or roommate requests.
[ ]   Invite additional staff, faculty and parents to the conference.
[ ]   Prepare your five-minute team presentation.
[ ]   Submit the name of your team rep for the opening ceremony.
[ ]   Email Lucas with copies of lessons for the multicultural curriculum bank.
[ ]   Bring any items you wish to display.

UnityWorks friends relax during a break: Heidi Griffin, Randie Gottlieb, Sharon Harris, Jessica Karstetter and Tcharles Anders

Invitation to Special Guests
* Your reply is requested by May 4

Dear _____,

Thank you for your interest in learning more about the UnityWorks School Program. An overview of the Program is included below. I would also like to invite you or another representative from your office to be my personal guest at our annual Spring Multicultural Conference on May 28, in Yakima, WA (see flier attached).

At the conference, you will have an opportunity to meet the UnityWorks site teams—including the principals from our six participating schools, learn what the teams are doing at each school, and speak firsthand with the participants.

Conference highlights will include…

If you plan to attend, please register with Lucas Ortiz (509-865-1234 or OrtizLucas@ysd.org) by May 4, so we have an accurate count for lunch and conference materials.

I look forward to hearing from you.

Letter to Keynote Speaker

Dear _____,

We are delighted to confirm your participation as the keynote speaker for our upcoming UnityWorks Spring Conference. As you know, the event is scheduled for all day Thursday, May 28, at the Yakima School District Central Office, 123 N. 4th Street in Yakima. We are inviting teams from all 15 UnityWorks schools, as well as students, parents, school boards and superintendents from nearby districts, the City Council, and interested community members.

The conference theme is "Ripples of Change." A flier and a draft program are enclosed. Your keynote presentation is tentatively scheduled for 9:00–9:40 a.m. and you will be introduced by Dr. Alexa Smith, President of Harmony University. Please let me know by May 1st if you have a specific title for your talk. We also need a resume that can be filed with our Educational Service District, as they are offering continuing education clock hours for the conference.

Please make your own flight arrangements and forward the invoice or receipt to Lucas Ortiz at the address below. I'll plan to meet you at the airport and would be happy to provide hospitality or to make hotel arrangements for your visit if you'd prefer. Let me know when you plan to arrive, and feel free to call with any questions.

We are all looking forward to seeing you at the conference!

Letter to Presenters

Dear _____,

We are writing to invite you to serve as a workshop presenter for the UnityWorks Spring Multi-cultural Conference on May 28 (see attached flier and program). Based on your work with students and on recommendations from our site team leaders, we would like to suggest the following topic:

_____

Workshop sessions are tentatively scheduled for 10:00–11:00 a.m. and 1:30–2:30 p.m. (one hour each). Let us know if you have a preference for the morning or the afternoon session, or if you would be willing to present during both times.

In addition, we will need the exact title and a 1-2 sentence description of your workshop for the conference program, some brief biographical information, and a list of any audiovisual equipment you might require. You should also include any handouts you would like us to copy for the participants.

While our limited budget does not allow us to offer speaking fees for this presentation, we would be happy to pay your travel expenses. We also invite you to join us for lunch and to attend the rest of the conference as our guest.

Please review the enclosed guidelines for presenters, and feel free to call with any questions.

We look forward to seeing you at the conference!

Letter to Sponsors

Dear _____,

We are writing to express our sincere thanks for your generous support of the UnityWorks School Program, and to invite you to join us as our guest at the Spring Conference on May 28 (see flier and program attached). Our seventeen participating schools are carrying out a wide variety of successful multicultural programs and activities which will be showcased at this event.

During lunch, we plan to honor all of our sponsors with a brief presentation, and we invite you to say a few words at that time. If you are planning to attend, please RSVP to Lucas Ortiz (865-1234 or OrtizLucas@ysd.org) at your earliest convenience.

Once again, we thank you for your support of this successful grassroots effort to build bridges of understanding among the diverse groups in our community.

We couldn't do it without you!

Letter of Confirmation to All Participants

Dear _____,

We are pleased to confirm your registration for the UnityWorks Spring Conference at the Yakima School District Office on May 28. Your registration includes a light lunch and afternoon snack. If you have special dietary needs or if you prefer to bring your own food, there is a refrigerator and microwave available. If you need to cancel, let us know as soon as possible so we can order the correct number of meals and conference materials.

Please be prepared for your team presentation, and remember to bring any materials you wish to display. During the conference, we hope to take some photos of the participants as well as your team's showcase items.

We plan to start promptly at 11:30 a.m., so please arrive 15-20 minutes early to park, sign in, and mingle with the other teams. There is free street parking around the building.

For those who are interested in continuing education clock hours, please sign the clock hour form at the registration desk when you arrive, and sign out again at the end of the day. Payment of $2/clock hour may be made online to ESD 105 after the event.

If you have any questions, please contact Lucas Ortiz (865-1234 or OrtizLucas@ysd.org).

We look forward to seeing you on May 28!

UnityWorks staff, site team members and students from Yakima, WA

Sample Guidelines

Guidelines for Registrars

Thank you for agreeing to assist with this important task!

1. Before people arrive

    a. Neatly set out any sign-in sheets, media releases, clock hour forms, name tags, handouts and other registration materials.

    b. Name tags can be sorted alphabetically and arranged into groups (e.g. A-L and M-Z), or organized by school or organization.

2. When someone enters

    a. <u>If they are on the list as paid</u>, check off their name. [√]

    b. <u>If they are on the list but haven't paid</u>, collect $20, or $10 for students with current ID.
- Checks should be payable to "YSD Special Programs."
- Be sure checks are signed, and write the check number next to their name on the list.
- If paying with cash, indicate the amount paid and write "cash" next to their name.
- Give a receipt for cash if they want one.

    c. <u>If they are not on the list</u>, add them (print name, organization, position) and collect the fee.

    d. <u>Make sure all sign the media release</u>, or if they do not wish to have their picture taken, give them a red sticker to place on their name tag, so the photographer will know.

    e. <u>If they want clock hours</u>, have them sign the form and remind them to sign out at the end.

    f. <u>Give everyone a name tag</u>, a conference program and handout packet, and let them know that the name tag will also be their lunch ticket.

3. Close the registration area after the keynote presentation.

    a. Leave the printed name tags spread out on the table in alphabetical order.

    b. Count up cash and checks, write totals on the envelope, sign and seal.

    c. Give all blank name tags, sign-in lists and money to Lucas Ortiz.

Guidelines for Hosts

Thank you for agreeing to assist with this important task!

1. Find and greet your assigned guest. Most should arrive at lunchtime.

2. Make them feel welcome and show them to their reserved table at the front.

3. Sit with them during the conference and answer any questions they might have.

Enjoy the conference!

Guidelines for Introducers

Thank you for agreeing to assist with this important task!

1. Meet briefly with the presenters and performers before their session to make them feel welcome and to find out a few things about them to share with the group.

2. When it's time, call the session to order and briefly introduce them to the group.

3. Let them know when there's about five minutes left, and thank them at the end.

Enjoy the conference!

Guidelines for Moderators

The MC or master of ceremonies plays a vital role in setting the tone and pace of the conference, and managing the content. Your primary job is to make everyone feel welcome and included, and then to keep the program moving forward in a timely manner. A good moderator will have the skill and confidence to effectively manage the speakers and the program, as well as handling any unexpected events. In addition to modeling energy and enthusiasm, duties may include:

- Welcome the audience.
- State the title and purpose of each session or activity.
- Introduce the presenters and performers.
- Engage the audience and encourage discussion on the topic at hand.
- Explain how questions will be handled, and facilitate Q&A sessions.
- Keep the program moving forward in a lively manner without feeling rushed.
- Maintain an environment that is courteous, respectful and kind.
- Start and end on time.

In a large auditorium, it may be helpful to use a bell or hand signal to bring the group back together after a discussion or breakout activity. The moderator may also need to assist with room setup, test the lights and microphones, and make sure any other audiovisual equipment is working properly.

Advance Preparation

Effective moderators don't just show up; they prepare beforehand. For example:

- Learn about the speakers and the audience, their areas of experience and points of view.
- Know something about the topic: key issues, terms and acronyms, areas of controversy.
- Confirm the time, date, place, format and other details with each presenter.
- Formulate some insightful questions to get the conversation rolling. For example, if moderating a panel you might prepare two or three concise questions for each panelist based on their field of expertise.
- Consider engaging the audience by asking for questions or taking a poll using index cards, social media, or technology like sli.do.
- Prepare strong opening and closing remarks.

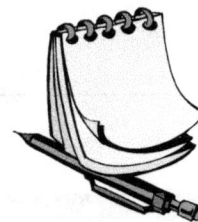

For Panel Discussions

The moderator should ensure that the discussion is relevant, engaging and worthwhile for the audience. A few practical tips:

- Keep your welcome and introductions short and to the point.
- Share any ground rules (e.g. courtesy, honesty, approximately five minutes each).
- Start the conversation, then stay out of the way when things are going well.
- Don't promote yourself, your company, your products or services.
- Adopt an inclusive, non-confrontational approach focused on learning.
- Bring out diverse points of view and ask questions to clarify as necessary.
- Probe beneath the surface, asking about specifics rather than generalities.

- Listen intently so you can effectively guide the conversation forward.
- Repeat any questions from the audience so everyone can hear them clearly.
- Balance panelist participation so that no one person dominates.
- If the conversation feels unbalanced, the moderator can say,
  "I wonder what the other panelists think about this," or
  "Let's take a moment to think about the question before jumping in."
- Intervene respectfully as needed to keep the session on topic and on time.
- Leave about one fourth of the panel's total time for Q&A.
- Synthesize the discussion and thank the participants at the end.

Near the end of the conference, in addition to thanking the hosts, sponsors, speakers and performers, the MC might let the audience know that thank-you cards are being circulated for all to sign. They should sign quickly and pass them on.

* * * * *

Guidelines for Presenters

Planning the Presentation

Whether you are a first-time presenter or one with years of experience, advance preparation will help your talk go more smoothly. Consider the following points:

1. Prepare a strong introduction that motivates the audience and captures their interest. You might start with a question, a demonstration or dramatic story. For example, Henry Ward Beecher began a speech against slavery by auctioning off a white slave girl with her hands tied behind her back.

2. Plan your presentation with the audience in mind:
   - What are they going to learn?
   - Why is it important? Why should the audience care about the topic?
   - Why should they listen to you? What are your relevant qualifications and experience?
   - What specific knowledge, skills, resources or tools will they gain?
   - What concerns might they have and what questions might they ask?
   - What actions can they take in response to your presentation?

3. Don't pack too much information into your talk. It's better to convey a few key messages, then repeat them several times. Additional details can be included in a handout. For example, begin with an attention-grabbing introduction followed by an outline of the main points you plan to present. Then deliver your presentation, summarize the main points, and end with impact.

4. Draw on real experiences, both positive and negative. Others can learn from your mistakes and challenges, and how you handled them.

5. You can add impact and emphasize the main points through the use of music, poetry, drama, short quotations, case studies, thought-provoking data, questions, visual aids, stories, sound effects or other techniques. Even silence can be used for dramatic effect. Don't overdo it, however. One or two of these techniques may be sufficient for a short talk.

6. Don't memorize your speech or read from a script. It is usually preferable to refer to index cards with a few keywords and images to remind you of the main points you wish to convey.

7. To ensure that you stay within the time limit, identify several check points within your presentation. For example, in a 30-minute talk, know what you want to have covered at 10, 15 and 25 minutes, so you can adjust the pace, eliminate portions of the talk, or take additional questions from the audience.

8. Engage the participants in an active learning experience. Depending on the time available, plan some participatory activities, including paired or small group discussions to help them process the material and share their own ideas.

9. Practice the presentation until it feels smooth and comfortable, staying within the time limit—including time for questions at the end.

AV Equipment, Visual Aids and Handouts

Simple graphs, photos, and other visual aids can clarify and enhance your message. Visual aids should be large enough for all to see. Include people from diverse backgrounds in the images as appropriate. When pointing to a chart, poster, map or other object, stand to the side so the audience has a clear view.

If you are planning to show a PowerPoint or video, bring it on your laptop with a backup copy on a thumb drive. Check with the facility to be sure your software will run on the computer in the room you have been assigned, and that there are sufficient outlets and extension cords, or a power strip to accommodate the necessary equipment. Have a backup plan in case of equipment failure. If you will distribute handouts, be sure enough copies are available.

PowerPoint Tips

PowerPoint is a tool that should only be used if it adds value to your presentation. A well-designed slide deck can capture the audience's attention, reinforce the spoken message, get your point across more effectively, and enhance retention by presenting information in an ordered way. It can also highlight key points, help the audience to visualize complex relationships, show photographs of an event, graphically illustrate statistics, and appeal to multiple learning styles.

A poorly done PowerPoint, on the other hand, can alienate the audience by reducing the presentation to an illegible mass of text or a tedious series of bullet points. The following tips may be of assistance:

1. Keep it Simple
   - Visuals should be clear and the text easy to read.
   - Well-designed, clearly-labeled graphs and diagrams are more easily understood.
   - Slides should have a limited amount of text, e.g., a single sentence or a few bullet points.
   - The letters should be large enough to read easily in the room you will use (at least 24 points).
   - Sans serif type (e.g. Arial or Tahoma) with upper and lower case lettering is more legible.
   - Maintain the same typeface from slide to slide, unless varying it for specific effect.
   - Too many different colors, styles and graphics can distract from your message.
   - It's also better to keep important content away from the slide edges in case something is blocking a corner of the screen, or the projected image is slightly larger than the screen and you can't reach the projector to adjust it.

2. Color Scheme
   - Use contrasting colors for the text and background (e.g. dark blue background with white text).
   - Avoid extremely bright or cluttered backgrounds that compete with the text.
   - Maintain a consistent color scheme throughout the presentation.

3. How Many Slides?
   - Use the number of slides needed to clearly and efficiently communicate your ideas.
   - This will depend on the length of your presentation and the complexity of the content.
   - The common "one slide per minute" rule doesn't take into account the amount of information on each slide. Some slides may flash on the screen for a few seconds; others may remain for several minutes while the speaker explains a process or describes an event.
   - Place extra slides at the end of the deck, so they can be used if time permits.

4. <u>During the Presentation</u>
- Don't just read aloud from the text on your slides, but talk directly to the audience.
- To jump forward or backward to a particular slide, type the slide number and press "enter."
- To darken the screen and pause the presentation, press "b" for "black."
- To resume, press "b" again.

You can also look online for more "PowerPoint design and delivery tips" and search Google images for "Steve Jobs presentation slides" to see some outstanding examples of attention-grabbing simplicity.

Before the Presentation

Arrive early to familiarize yourself with the room and to check arrangements in advance (microphone, sound system, projector and screen, whiteboard, flip chart, markers, location of outlets, lighting, seating, etc.). Practice with the equipment beforehand, and do a sound check if using a microphone. You should also introduce yourself to the session chair.

During the Presentation

1. Engage the audience with memorable opening and closing lines.

2. Develop a connection with your audience. Begin with a greeting and imagine that you are talking to one or two individuals, not a faceless mass. Don't stand behind the podium the entire time. If culturally appropriate, make eye contact with people around the room.

3. Speak with conviction and enthusiasm, using a melodious voice rather than a monotone. A strong voice and clear pronunciation will enable people at the back of the room to hear and understand you. Maintain a moderate speed without rushing through your talk.

4. Minimize the use of fill words (well, um, like, you know). Use technical terms and acronyms as appropriate, and explain them as needed.

5. Be aware of posture, hand and body movements. If using a microphone, hold it close enough and at an angle that will clearly capture and carry your voice. You can find additional tips for using a microphone by searching online for "microphone tips for public speaking."

6. Ask questions of the audience to encourage participation and keep them engaged. You can search "asking audience questions" for specific ideas.

7. Repeat any questions from the audience so everyone can hear, and answer to the best of your ability. If you don't know, say that you don't know but will try to find out, or ask if someone in the audience has the answer. If a question is obviously of little interest to the participants, or takes you too far off topic, politely offer to discuss it with that person after your talk.

8. Don't apologize for your speech or your speaking ability.

9. Enjoy the presentation!

My Story Presentations

Everyone has a story. Participants from previous UnityWorks trainings and conferences have stated that the "My Story" presentations are the most meaningful part of the event. This sharing of personal histories can increase understanding and create bridges between those of diverse backgrounds, an important step in breaking down barriers between people.

If possible, select presenters from a variety of backgrounds. Explain that the purpose of their presentation is to allow the participants to meet them as individuals rather than as the representative of an entire racial, religious, ethnic or other group. We usually give speakers 30 minutes for their talk, plus 15 minutes for questions and answers. The following guidelines (also available in the download packet) can be given in advance to those who have agreed to share their stories.

Some previous "My Story" presenters. From top left: Mary Looney, Victor Nourani, Maria "Zuky" Alvarado. From bottom left: Mako Nakagawa, Maria Cuevas, Tcharles Anders.

"MY STORY"

Presentation for UnityWorks Spring Conference

Thank you for agreeing to share your story! We know you have taken time from a busy schedule and this is truly appreciated. The purpose of your presentation is to allow the participants to meet you as an individual—not as the representative of an entire racial, religious, ethnic or other group. This sharing of personal histories can increase understanding and create bridges between those of diverse backgrounds, an important step in breaking down barriers between people.

The participants, many of whom are teachers, would also like to learn about your school experience, so they might make positive changes for the students in their own classrooms. The goal is not to praise or blame, but to learn how our attitudes and practices affect students and their families, and how we can improve together.

Your presentation should be about ___ minutes long, followed by ___ minutes for questions and answers. If you have any objects, maps, photos, music, artwork, clothing or other items that are meaningful to your story, please feel free to share them with the group. In addition, you may wish to include some of the following information.

- **Personal history and experiences**
  - Birthplace, family and ancestors
  - Early life, schooling, work, travel, marriage, children, service
  - Experiences that helped develop your own identity and understanding of others

- **Information about your racial, religious, ethnic or other group**
  - Historical information
  - Diversity within your group
  - Customs, traditions, values, special observances
  - Current issues and challenges, opportunities and dreams

- **School experiences and suggestions for educators**

Your presentation is scheduled for:

Date: _____   Time: _____

Place: _____

Please contact _____ **with any questions:** _____

Conference Evaluation

Conference Evaluation Form

Location: _____   Date: _____

Please answer the following questions and drop your completed form in the Evaluation Box.
Use the reverse side if needed. Your frank assessment will help us to improve future programs.

HIGH ←——→ LOW

	PLEASE RATE THE FOLLOWING	5	4	3	2	1	Comments
1	Advance publicity						
2	Facility						
3	Meals and refreshments						
4	Organization of the conference						
5	Content of the program						
6	Pace of the schedule						
7	Speaker 1:						
8	Speaker 2:						
9	Panel presentation						
10	Cultural performance						
11	Benefit to you and your work						
12	Benefit to your team or organization						

I liked: _____

_____

I learned: _____

_____

I suggest: _____

_____

Other comments: _____

_____

_____

Your position: [ ] Teacher   [ ] Administrator   [ ] Student   [ ] Other: _____

THANK YOU!

Additional Resources
and Notes

Additional Resources

UnityWorks is pleased to offer the following resources in support of your efforts to promote understanding of the oneness of humanity, the value of diversity and the need for unity.

> **Visit our online bookstore for more information: www.unityworks.org**

UnityWorks Books

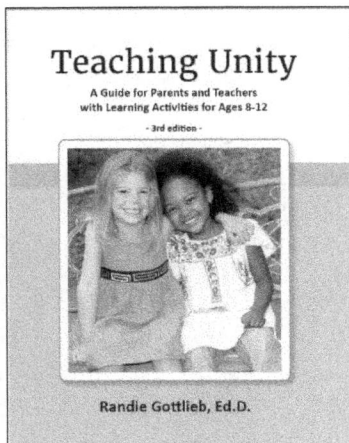

Teaching Unity
A Guide for Parents and Teachers
Author: Randie Gottlieb
ISBN: 978-1-942053-09-5
309 pages, paperback

Designed for use with ages 8-12, this easy-to-use, award-winning curriculum package contains a treasury of fun, hands-on learning activities on Unity, Diversity, Skin Color and Overcoming Prejudice. Four colorful PowerPoint programs for kids and copy-ready student handouts are included.

"A book that should be adopted throughout the United States. Warmest congratulations on this important contribution to bringing about the unity of mankind."
— Judge Dorothy W. Nelson, U.S. Federal Court of Appeals

Teaching Unity has more great ideas on one page than some books do in the whole volume!
— Dr. Stephanie Eijsink, M.D., First Physicians Clinic, East Texas Medical Center

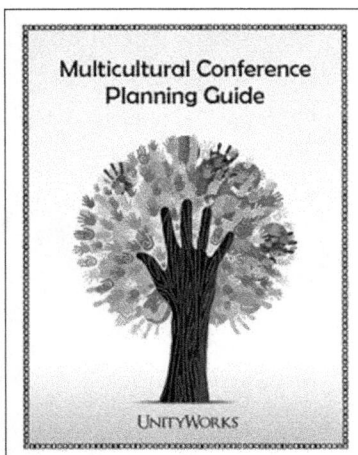

Multicultural Conference Planning Guide
Author: Randie Gottlieb
ISBN: 978-1-942053-03-3
60 pages, paperback

This handbook is designed to assist with planning a multicultural conference. It includes theme and program ideas, sample letters of invitation, fliers, schedules, recommendations for room setup, guidelines for moderators and presenters, registration instructions, a planning checklist, an evaluation form and other essential materials.

PowerPoint Programs

One Human Race
PowerPoint #1
48 slides, download

This colorful slide show introduces the idea that people are alike and different in many ways, but there is only one human race, and we all share one planet—our common home. Also available in Russian and Spanish.

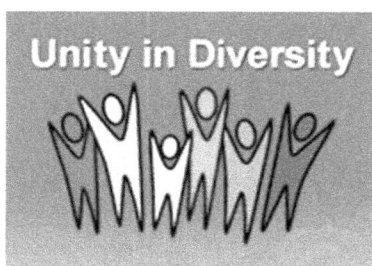

Unity in Diversity
PowerPoint #2
61 slides, download

This slide show compares the members of our human family to the flowers of a garden, each with its own special beauty. It also considers the value of diversity, the need for unity, and the difference between unity and sameness.

The Colors We Are
PowerPoint #3
37 slides, download

This program takes a close look at the variation in human skin colors, the problems with labeling people by color, how skin color is inherited from our parents, and the role of melanin in protecting us from the sun.

Teaching Unity
PowerPoint #4
27 slides, download

This colorful slide show reviews concepts from the first three programs on One Human Race, Diversity, and The Colors We Are. It also poses discussion questions to encourage deeper thinking.

Overcoming Prejudice
PowerPoint #5
53 slides, download

This show makes it easy to talk with children and others about prejudice. Topics include a simple definition of prejudice with concrete examples, ways to overcome prejudice and create unity, and discussion questions to encourage deeper thinking.

What People Are Saying

"I LOVE this new PowerPoint. It even brought tears to my eyes."
— Dr. Susan Walker, Middle School Teacher, Seattle, WA

"Thank you so much for the lessons and PowerPoints on Unity!
This is going to help more than you can think."
— Alem Hamzik, Youth Leadership Program, Bosnia

"We have downloaded all the power point presentations and they are wonderful!
'So powerful is the light of unity, it can illumine the whole earth.'
What greater service can one give."
— Cynthia Catches, Project Director, OCETI WAKAN,
Sacred Fireplace, Pine Ridge, South Dakota

"Brilliant and lotsa fun!
You may have designed it for kids but adults would benefit too!"
— Aggie Toyoda, Yakima, WA

"The power points are excellent. The more these are in the hands of the friends,
the more they will feel confident to lift up their voices and share the potent messages
you have captured in these presentations. You are producing the stuff we need!"
— Bob Harris, Florida

School Climate Survey

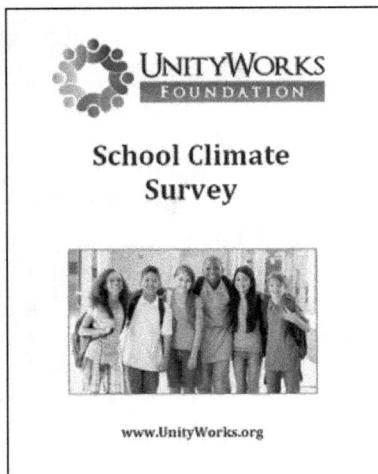

UNITYWORKS
FOUNDATION

**School Climate
Survey**

www.UnityWorks.org

**35 pages
PDF and Word format
for easy editing**

This ready-made Survey is designed for use by state departments of education, school districts and local schools. It focuses on multicultural attitudes and practices, with questions about school culture, curriculum, instruction, classroom materials, after-school activities and parent involvement, as well as student-student and student-teacher interactions.

The package includes staff and student questionnaires, sample cover letters, instructions for survey administration, focus group questions, parent interview questions in English and Spanish, and an example of survey results.

What People Are Saying

"The survey itself was very informative and educational for our staff."
"It helped tremendously with staff buy-in to multicultural education."
"It is affecting everything we're doing in a more conscious way."
"Just doing this survey has already made positive changes in our school."

Conversations on Race

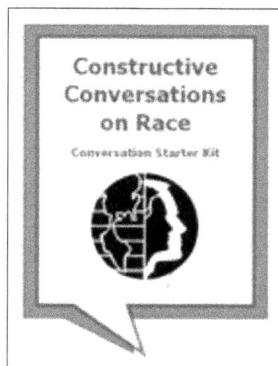

Constructive Conversations on Race
Conversation Starter Kit
15 pages, PDF download

This easy-to-use conversation starter kit contains basic guidelines and structured activities for facilitating conversations about race with family, friends, neighbors, classmates, co-workers, and community groups.

The materials are carefully designed to promote understanding, so that participants feel free to express their views in a full and frank manner, but with courtesy, moderation and respect.

"Constructive Conversations on Race is a proven program that has led to many healthy, non-accusatory discussions on race, and to a significant number of interracial/-congregational friendships that are continuing to blossom across the Springfield, IL area." — Springfield Race Unity Committee

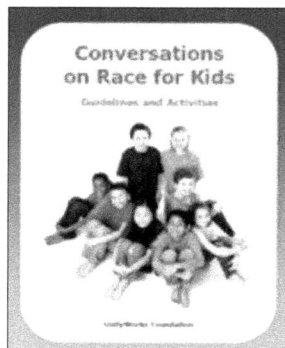

Conversations on Race for Kids
Guidelines and Activities
32 pages, PDF download

This booklet is a resource for parents and teachers for talking with children about race. Children need a safe environment to share their experiences, questions and concerns, and to discuss positive ways to respond to prejudice and promote unity.

Designed for use with ages 8-12, the booklet is organized around four themes: Our Similarities and Differences, Skin Color, Personal Stories, and Overcoming Prejudice. The activities, adapted from our Teaching Unity curriculum, include discussion questions, poems, songs, and four colorful PowerPoints available separately.

Overcoming Prejudice
To Parents and Teachers
2 pages, free PDF download

Many young children already hold negative stereotypes of other racial and ethnic groups by the time they enter first grade.

Parents and teachers can help to reduce prejudice by talking about it directly with children. We can encourage children to work side-by-side with those from other backgrounds. We can serve as role models.

We can also give them the tools and strategies needed to form healthy attitudes and relationships, and we can plan specific activities that foster cooperation and understanding.

What People Are Saying

"I am absolutely thrilled to hear of your new publication. Your valuable work in this area is such an assistance to so many parents."
— Layli Miller-Muro, Founder and Executive Director, Tahirih Justice Center

"Very impressive. I like the conversation starter kit's simplicity. The steps are clear and easy to follow, and this will help people discuss a complex and emotional topic. The format allows for small group sharing, large group discussion, opportunities to learn what the science tells us about race, time to problem-solve and brainstorm steps for future action. Well done!"
— Dr. Susan Walker, Middle School Teacher

More Resources

Portraits of Humanity
Color photographs
48-pages, PDF download

You'll love this color photo collection with 45 stunning portraits of our brothers and sisters from around the world. These full-page photos may be viewed on a computer screen, projected, printed and laminated or framed and mounted on the wall. Perfect for decorating your home or classroom. Great for talking with students about the oneness of humanity and the beauty of our diversity.

We Are Drops
Video and song sheet
36 MB, .wmv file + PDF
FREE

Also known as the Hawaiian Unity Song. Children will love singing along with this 3-minute animated video, as they learn that we are all drops of one ocean, leaves of one tree, and flowers of one garden. The video was produced by Houcein Oualil of Morocco.

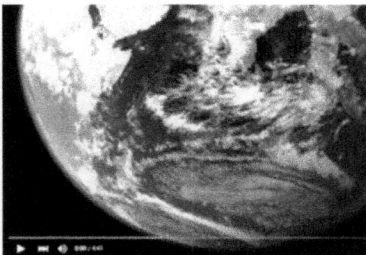

Wage Peace
Music video (5 min.)
Music & lyrics, Bill Fagan
Vocals, Mary Rebmann

This inspirational video uses beautiful images and simple lyrics to help us understand that "the sun shines on all, great and small" and that we should "wage peace not war, that's what we're fighting for" because "the earth we share is one."

Notes

_____

_____

_____

_____

_____

_____

_____

_____

_____

_____

_____

_____

_____

_____

_____

_____

_____

_____

_____

_____

_____

_____

_____

_____

_____

_____

_____

_____

www.ingramcontent.com/pod-product-compliance
Lightning Source LLC
Chambersburg PA
CBHW062054090426
42740CB00016B/3132

* 9 7 8 1 9 4 2 0 5 3 0 3 3 *